by
Peggy Beauregard
and
Crystal McCoppin

with illustrations by **Martha Moore**

ISBN 978-1717177179
www.ChooseHappyBook.com
by Peggy Beauregard and Crystal McCoppin
Illustrations by Martha Moore

Design & layout, McMAC Publications
Mammoth Lakes, CA 93546

©2018
No part of this publication may be reproduced
in any way without prior written permission.

Make someone happy
...gift them this book!

Sweet happy Sara!
Grateful to know you —
inspired by
your warmth, your
amazing jewelry!,
your survivorship ☺,
your contributions
to all your passions,
& your love of
movies
& of course
[illegible] &
our love for
Jane ☺
XO Crystal

Remember...

"Life should not be a journey to the grave
with the intention of arriving safely
in an attractive and well-preserved body,
but rather to skid in sideways,
Champagne in one hand,
chocolate-covered strawberries in the other,
body thoroughly used up,
worn out, and screaming
'WooHoo, what a ride!'."

Variation of a quote by
Hunter S. Thompson

Life is full of choices
...choose wisely

"When one door of happiness closes,
another opens; but often we look so long
at the closed door that we do not see
the one which has been opened for us."
Helen Keller

"The pessimist complains about the wind;
the optimist expects it to change;
the realist adjusts the sails."
William A. Ward

Relax in the bubbles

"We often fantasize about a perfect day –
something exotic and far away. But when it
comes to those we miss, we desperately want
one more meal, even one more argument.
What does this teach us?
That the ordinary is precious.
That the normal day is a treasure."
Mitch Albom

"My guilty pleasure is a deep, eco-unfriendly,
hot bath. Preferably with a glass of champagne
and someone sitting on the loo seat gossiping."
Prue Leith

Seek moments

"Live from the heart of yourself.
Seek to be whole, not perfect."
Oprah Winfrey

"If an egg is broken by an outside force, life
ends. If broken by an inside force, life begins.
Great things always begin from the inside."
Jim Kwik

"If you get the inside right,
the outside will fall into place."
Eckhart Tolle

Be a hugger

"You can't wrap love in a box,
but you can wrap a person in a hug."
Anonymous

"A kiss without a hug
is like a flower without the fragrance."
Proverb

"A hug is like a boomerang
- you get it back right away."
Bil Keane

Pay it forward

"Sometimes small things are the ones
one is grateful for all through life. At a faculty
reception a British lady taught me how to tie
my shoes with a double knot so that they keep
tied more securely and still come apart in a jiffy.
Kneeling on the floor in the midst of the
chattering sherry-sippers she tied my shoes.
I remember her twice a day ever since."

Rudolf Arnheim

Acknowledge your assets

"One of the great responsibilities that I have
is to manage my assets wisely,
so that they create value."
Alice Walton

"It's not about the dress you wear,
but it's about the life you lead in the dress."
Diana Vreeland

"I say, dress to please yourself.
Listen to your inner muse and take a chance.
Wear something that says 'Here I am' today."
Iris Apfel

Share something sweet

Create an aroma of love, joy and memories.

"We cannot do great things on this earth,
only small things with great love."
Mother Teresa

"A party without cake is just a meeting."
Julia Child

"Music I heard with you was more than music,
And bread I broke with you
was more than bread."
Conrad Aiken

Energize at a concert under the stars

"A live concert to me is exciting because
of all the electricity that is generated
in the crowd and on stage.
It's my favorite part of the business,
live concerts."
Elvis Presley

"If I should ever die, God forbid,
let this be my epitaph:
The only proof he needed
for the existence of God was music."
Kurt Vonnegut

"Give me books, French wine, fruit,
fine weather and a little music played
out of doors by somebody I do not know."
J. Keats

Love what you do

"Success is not the key to happiness.
Happiness is the key to success. If you love
what you are doing, you will be successful."
Albert Schweitzer

"Your work is going to fill a large part of your
life, and the only way to be truly satisfied is to
do what you believe is great work. And the only
way to do great work is to love what you do."
Steve Jobs

"When you are inspired by some great purpose,
some extraordinary project, all your thoughts
break their bounds. Your mind transcends
limitations, your consciousness expands in
every direction and you find yourself in a new,
great and wonderful world. Dormant forces,
faculties and talents become alive, and you
discover yourself to be a greater person by far
than you ever dreamed yourself to be."
Patanjali

"The secret of joy in work is contained in
one word - excellence. To know how to do
something well is to enjoy it."
Pearl S. Buck

"If you observe a really happy man
you will find him building a boat,
writing a symphony, educating his son,
growing Double Dahlias in his garden."
W. Beran Wolfe

"He was caught in a rare moment
of contentment that did not depend
on the moment that would follow."
Anne Roiphe

Discover your talents

"Go deep and live life from your truth within,
and watch your most authentic self,
full of love, peace, and beauty
manifest out into the world."
D. S. Clark

Be courageous...go for it!

"Courage is not having the strength to go on;
it is going on when you don't have the strength."
Theodore Roosevelt

"Faith is taking the first step,
even when you don't see the whole staircase."
Martin Luther King, Jr.

"Courage is what it takes to stand up and speak.
Courage is also what it takes
to sit down and listen."
Winston Churchill

Be present
to how good you feel

"I don't have any better sense than to be happy."
Dave McCoy, Mammoth Mountain founder

Go dog go!

"In order to really enjoy a dog,
one doesn't merely try and train it
to be semihuman. The point of it is
to open oneself to the possibility
of becoming partly a dog."
Edward Hoagland

"If you can sit quietly after difficult news,
if in financial downturns you remain perfectly calm,
if you can see your neighbors travel to fantastic
places without a twinge of jealousy,
if you can happily eat whatever is put on your
plate, and fall asleep after a day of running around
without a drink or a pill, if you can always find
contentment just where you are,
you are probably a dog."
Jack Kornfield

Enjoy a walk
under the full moon

"The night walked down the sky
with the moon in her hand."
Frederick L. Knowles

"From now on we live in a world
where man has walked on the moon.
It's not a miracle; we just decided to go."
Tom Hanks

"And if you're ever feeling lonely
just look at the moon…
someone, somewhere is looking right at it too."
Unknown

Puzzle me this

"There are no extra pieces in the universe.
Everyone is here because he or she has a place to fill,
and every piece must fit itself into the big jigsaw puzzle."
Deepak Chopra

"You cannot be lonely if you like the person
you're alone with."
Wayne Dyer

"Golf is a puzzle without an answer.
I've played the game for 40 years and I still haven't
the slightest idea how to play."
Gary Player

Today's game plan:
encourage others

"Beacon: a light source of guidance or inspiration...
someone or something that gives HOPE to others.
Who are our beacons?
How can we be a beacon?"
Unknown

"When we decide to be happy
we accept the responsibility
to bring happiness to someone else.
Some decide that happiness and glee
are the same thing, they are not.
When we choose happiness we accept
the responsibility to lighten the load
of someone else and be a light on the path
to another who may be walking in darkness."
Maya Angelou

"Why not invest your assets
in the companies you really like?
As Mae West said,
'Too much of a good thing can be wonderful'."
Warren Buffett

Bring the cheer

"The best way to cheer yourself up
is to try to cheer somebody else up."
Mark Twain

"A cheerful look brings joy to the heart."
William Makepeace Thackeray

"Cheerfulness and contentment
are great beautifiers
and are famous preservers of youthful looks."
Charles Dickens

"The noblest art is that of making others happy."
P.T. Barnum

Make a new friend
...kids do this easily

"Another plan I have is World Peace through
Formal Introductions. The idea is that everyone
in the world would be required to meet everyone
else in the world, formally, at least once.
You'd have to look the person in the eye, shake
hands, repeat their name, and try to remember
one outstanding physical characteristic.
My theory is,
if you knew everyone in the world personally,
you'd be less inclined to fight them in a war:
Who? The Malaysians?
Are you kidding? I know those people!"

George Carlin

Positive thoughts bring positive actions and results

"Why do we say we're over the hill?
I don't even know what that means
and why it's a bad thing.
When I go hiking and I get over the hill,
that means I'm past the hard part
and there's a snack in my future."
Ellen Degeneres

"The ability to attain our goals,
to control our experiences and have them
result in happiness, prosperity and success,
lies within our own thinking
and the way we use it."
Betty Simmons, Coaching Magic

"A great attitude becomes a great mood;
a great mood becomes a great day,
a great day becomes a great year,
a great year becomes a great life."
Unknown

"Through his thoughts, man holds the key
to every situation and contains within himself
that transforming and regenerative agency
by which he may make himself what he wills."
James Allen

Savory sips with a buddy

"A lot of harmony can be brought
into a relationship over a good cup of chai.
Our hearts and minds have
completely different functions to perform
and often compliment each other."
Vish Iyer, 'Yoga and Love'

"There is nothing better than a friend,
unless it is a friend with chocolate."
Charles Dickens

Widen your circle

"And in the end
The love you take
Is equal to the love you make"
Lennon-McCartney

"The circles of women around us weave
invisible nets of love that carry us when we're
weak and sing with us when we're strong."
Sark

"The planet does not need more successful
people. The planet desperately needs more
peacemakers, healers, restorers,
storytellers and lovers of all kinds."
Dalai Lama

"Love isn't a state of perfect caring.
It is an active noun like struggle.
To love someone is to strive to accept
that person exactly the way he or she is,
right here and now."
Fred Rogers

Dream ... **big,** small,
and everything in between

"You are never too old to set another goal
or to dream a new dream."
C.S. Lewis

"You control your future, your destiny.
What you think about comes about.
By recording your dreams and goals on paper,
you set in motion the process of becoming
the person you most want to be.
Put your future in good hands - your own."
Mark Victor Hansen

Break trail
...do something completely new

"Some amazing things are in faraway places,
some are down the road, and sometimes
the amazing thing is just the road itself."
Mark Parent

"No pleasure endures unseasoned by variety."
Publilius Syrus

Make a movie date
...don't forget the popcorn

"Imagination is everything.
It is the preview of life's coming attractions."
Albert Einstein

"I like nonsense, it wakes up the brain cells.
Fantasy is a necessary ingredient in living,
it's a way of looking at life through
the wrong end of a telescope.
Which is what I do, and that
enables you to laugh at life's realities."
Dr. Seuss

Give generously

"We make a living by what we get,
we make a life by what we give."
Sir Winston Churchill

"That's what I consider true generosity:
you give your all, and yet you always feel
as if it costs you nothing."
Simone de Beauvoir

Happy dance
...let your heart light shine

"The dog's tail wagged.
It was his tail's job:
to synchronize all nearby moods
to the measure of his joy.
A metronome of happiness."
Unknown

"Believe in the magic of tomorrow
and your spirits will be lifted on wings of hope."
Kobi Yamada

Find your rhythm

"If music be the food of love, play on,
give me excess of it."
William Shakespeare

"One good thing about music,
when it hits you, you feel no pain."
Bob Marley

"Where words fail, music speaks."
Hans Christian Andersen

Stop and smell those roses

"Let us be grateful to people who make us happy,
they are the charming gardeners
who make our souls blossom."
Marcel Proust

Keep it yummy

"Vegetables are a must on a diet.
I suggest carrot cake,
zucchini bread, and pumpkin pie."
Jim Davis

"Trail mix is M&M's with obstacles."
Unknown

"You better cut the pizza in four pieces
because I'm not hungry enough to eat six."
Yogi Berra

Push beyond your boundaries

"If you hear a voice within you say
'you cannot paint', then by all means paint,
and that voice will be silenced."
Vincent Van Gogh

"Without deviation from the norm,
progress is not possible."
Frank Zappa

"Have patience!
In time, even grass becomes milk."
Charan Singh

Finding frozen fun

"If you are not a skater, you probably can't imagine what I mean. I could try to tell you by saying it's a feeling of ice miles running under your blades, the wind splitting open to let you through, the earth whirling around you....It's a sense of power, of command over distance and gravity, and an illusion of no longer having to move because movement is carrying you."

Sonja Henie

What's your sport?

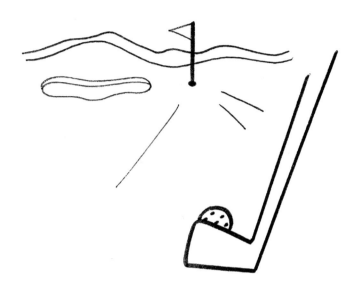

"The human body is the best work of art."
Jess C. Scott

"My goal is not to be better than anyone else,
but to be better than I used to be."
Dr. Wayne Dyer

"The most difficult thing is the decision to act.
The rest is merely tenacity."
Amelia Earhart

Surprise your taste buds

"Sandwiches are wonderful.
You don't need a spoon or a plate!"
Paul Lynde

"It's difficult to think anything but pleasant
thoughts while eating a homegrown tomato."
Lewis Grizzard

"Cheese - milk's leap toward immortality."
Clifton Fadiman

"If more of us valued food and cheer and song
above hoarded gold,
it would be a merrier world."
J.R.R. Tolkien

Tickle someone's feet
Of course!
(does it really have to be said?)

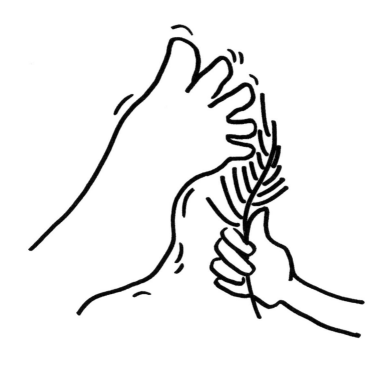

"Sometimes our light goes out,
but is blown again into instant flame
by an encounter with another human being."
Albert Schweitzer

"If you're going through hell, keep going."
Winston Churchill

Experience
the greatest of ease

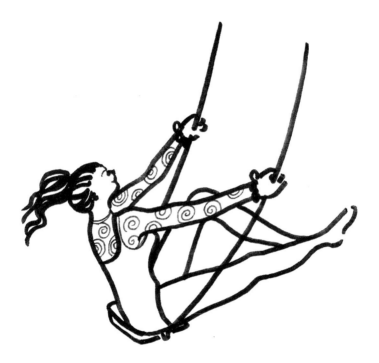

"The desire to fly is an idea handed down to us
by our ancestors who, in their grueling travels
across trackless lands in prehistoric times, looked
enviously on the birds soaring freely through space,
at full speed, above all obstacles,
on the infinite highway of the air."
Wilbur Wright

"An arrow can only be shot by pulling it
backward. When life is dragging you back
with difficulties, it means it's going to
launch you into something great.
So just focus, and keep aiming."
Author unknown

Find a quiet space
every day

"The outward work will never be puny
if the inward work is great."
Meister Eckhart

"…man's harmony is no more to be invaded
than the rhythm of the universe…"
Mary Baker Eddy

Wind is more fun with a kite

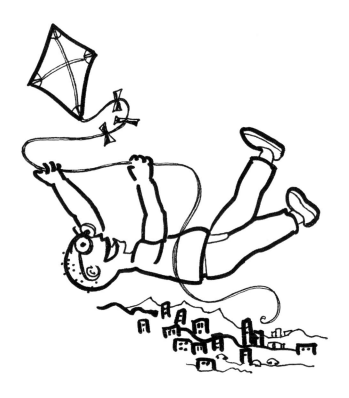

"Momentum," she repeats.
"You can't just stand there
if you want something to fly.
You have to run."
Lauren DeStefano

"When everything seems to be going
against you, remember that the airplane
takes off against the wind, not with it."
Henry Ford

Exercise...break a sweat

"To strengthen the mind
you must harden the muscles."
Michel Eyquem de Montaigne

"If you're trying to achieve, there will be roadblocks.
I've had them; everybody has had them.
But obstacles don't have to stop you.
If you run into a wall, don't turn around and give up.
Figure out how to climb it,
go through it, or work around it."
Michael Jordan

Snowflakes on your tongue

"Be happy for no reason, like a child.
If you are happy for a reason, you're in trouble,
because that reason can be taken from you."
Deepak Chopra

"The way to happiness: keep your heart
free from hate, your mind from worry.
Live simply, expect little, give much.
Scatter sunshine,
forget self, think of others.
Try this for a week and you will be surprised."
Norman Vincent Peale

Share your ideas...
what bounces back may be the nugget

"Daring ideas are like chessmen moved forward.
They may be beaten,
but they may start a winning game."
Johann Wolfgang von Goethe

"The whiter my hair becomes,
the more ready people are to believe what I say."
Bertrand Russell

"If you have an important point to make,
don't try to be subtle or clever.
Use a pile driver. Hit the point once.
Then come back and hit it again.
Then hit it a third time with a tremendous whack."
Winston Churchill

Mmm, ice cream

"I doubt whether the world holds for anyone
a more soul-stirring surprise
than the first adventure with ice cream
- happiness condensed."
Jessi Lane Adams

"Almost everything will work again
if you unplug it for a few minutes
…including you."
Anne Lamott

Beat the heat
...be silly, skip & hop & laugh

"Now I see the secret of making the best person.
It is to grow in the open air
and to eat and sleep with the earth."
Walt Whitman

"A day without sunshine is like, you know, night."
Steve Martin

"We all want to be a little glamorous, a little
playful and a little mischievous at times."
Jason Wu

Live with mirth

"I try to decorate my imagination
as much as I can."
Franz Schubert

"For all beings within this universal kingdom,
their magnetic north rests in genuine mirth."
Gabriel Brunsdon

"Laughter is eternity if joy is real."
Bono

Play in the waves
...life is better with sandy feet

"Surfing's one of the few sports that you
look ahead to see what's behind."
Laird Hamilton

"To change one's life: Start immediately.
Do it flamboyantly. No exceptions."
William James

"In the end, only three things matter: how much
you loved, how gently you lived, and how
gracefully you let go of things not meant for you."
Buddha

Make Pavarotti proud

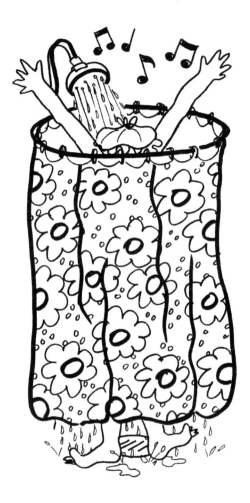

"There's no half-singing in the shower,
you're either a rock star or an opera diva."
Josh Groban

"You can cage the singer but not the song."
Harry Belafonte

Do nothing for several minutes

"Time goes, you say? Ah no!
Alas, time stays, we go."
Henry Austin Dobson

"Needing nothing attracts everything."
Russell Simmons

Everything you need
is here and available now

"Seize the moment.
Remember all those women on the Titanic
who waved off the dessert cart."
Erma Bombeck

"We can change our lives.
We can do, have, and be
exactly what we wish."
Tony Robbins

"The only courage you ever need
is the courage to live the life you want."
Oprah Winfrey

Ride!!

"May your trails be crooked, winding,
lonesome, dangerous, leading to the
most amazing view.
May your mountains rise into
and above the clouds."
Edward Abbey

"The whole world is a series of miracles,
but we're so used to seeing them that
we call them ordinary things."
Hans Christian Andersen

Sync a play date

"Don't walk behind me; I may not lead.
Don't walk in front of me; I may not follow.
Just walk beside me and be my friend."
Albert Camus

"Friendship is precious, not only in the shade,
but in the sunshine of life, and
thanks to a benevolent arrangement
the greater part of life is sunshine."
Thomas Jefferson

"If you want to have a good friend,
BE a good friend."
Dr. Phil

Give your "someone" a kiss

"A kiss is a lovely trick designed by nature to stop speech when words become superfluous."
Ingrid Bergman

"Any man who can drive safely while kissing a pretty girl is simply not giving the kiss the attention it deserves."
Albert Einstein

"A kiss that speaks volumes is seldom a first edition."
Clare Whiting

"A kiss, when all is said, what is it?
A rosy dot placed on the "i" in loving;
'Tis a secret told to the mouth instead of to the ear."
Edmond Rostand

Laugh 'til you cry

"The awkward moment when you're laughing
so hard, no noise comes out,
and you sit there clapping like a seal."
Anonymous

"Laughter gives us distance.
It allows us to step back from an event,
deal with it and then move on."
Bob Newhart

"My dog winks at me sometimes...
and I always wink back
in case it's some kind of code."
Unknown

Celebrate and spread joy

"Joy is what happens to us
when we allow ourselves to recognize
how good things really are."
Marianne Williamson

"Beauty is not in the face;
beauty is a light in the heart."
Kahil Gibran

Visit an aquarium...find Dory

"It is an important and popular fact that things are not always what they seem. For instance, on the planet Earth, man had always assumed that he was more intelligent than dolphins because he had achieved so much - the wheel, New York, wars and so on - whilst all the dolphins had ever done was muck about in the water having a good time. But conversely, the dolphins had always believed that they were far more intelligent than man - for precisely the same reasons."

Douglas Adams, 'The Hitch Hiker's Guide to the Galaxy'

Say "I love you"

"Was she so loved because her eyes were
so beautiful, or were her eyes so beautiful
because she was so loved?"
Anzia Yezierska

"Where there is love there is life."
Mahatma Gandhi

"Many people will walk in and out of your life,
but only true friends will leave
footprints in your heart."
Anonymous

Paint with whimsy

"You know you're an artist when you go through
the whole day with ink and paint smeared
across the left side of your face,
and when you find out, all you think is,
Wow, that's a cool pattern!"
Anonymous

"I am an artist. I paint with my fingers.
Texture makes me happy. I love drippage.
Building layers tells my story. I experience color.
I make mistakes beautiful.
I see what others cannot. I live inspired."
Donna Downey

Splish, splash

"We swim because we are too sexy
for a sport that requires clothes."
Anonymous

"Don't wait for your ship to come in,
swim out to it."
Anonymous

Find nirvana

"Paradise is exactly where you are right now,
only much, much better."
Laurie Anderson

"Be developed in ease and quiet.
Only through experience of trial
can the soul be strengthened,
ambition inspired and success achieved."
Helen Keller

'Quench'
on a hot summer's day

"He was a wise man who invented beer."
Plato

"Only one thing is certain about coffee...
wherever it is grown, sold, brewed,
and consumed, there will be lively controversy,
strong opinions, and good conversation."
Mark Pendergrast

"I come from a family
where gravy is considered a beverage."
Erma Bombeck

Honor the giver
with grateful acceptance

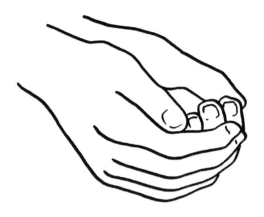

"The greatest gift of life is friendship,
and I have received it."
Hubert H. Humphrey

"My father gave me the greatest gift
anyone could give another person,
he believed in me."
Jim Valvano

"Friendship is the gift that goes on giving
and is a gift to both the person given to
and to the giver as well.
But to really make it work it isn't enough
to give to another person,
you have also to let them give to you."
Merle Shain

Get lost in a good book

"Each instant is a place we've never been."
Mark Strand

"Fantasy is escapist, and that is its glory.
If a soldier is imprisoned by the enemy,
don't we consider it his duty to escape?
If we value the freedom of mind and soul,
if we're partisans of liberty,
then it's our plain duty to escape,
and to take as many people with us as we can!"
J.R.R. Tolkien

"Good friends, good books,
and a sleepy conscience:
this is the ideal life."
Mark Twain

Risk a dazzling new look

"Hair brings one's self-image into focus;
it is vanity's proving ground. Hair is terribly
personal, a tangle of mysterious prejudices."
Shana Alexander

"My hair had grown out long and shaggy – not in
that sexy-young-rock-star kind of way but in that
time-to-take-Rover-to-the-groomer kind of way."
Jim Butcher, 'White Night'

"I'm not offended by all the dumb-blonde jokes
because I know that I'm not dumb.
I also know I'm not blonde"
Dolly Parton

Schedule lunch with a friend

"Friends are kisses blown to us by angels."
Author Unknown

"If I had a flower for every time
I thought of you...
I could walk through my garden forever."
Alfred Tennyson

"Good friends offer advice and wisdom.
Best friends come over unnaounced
with vodka, super hero costumes,
glitter, fireworks, and bacon."
Unknown

Simplify simplify simplify

Pass it on to someone who may need it
- keep only what you love

"Our life is frittered away by detail
…simplify, simplify."
Henry David Thoreau

"Don't agonize. Organize."
Florynce R. Kennedy

"The trouble with retirement is
you never get a day off!"
Abe Lemons

Seek amazing adventures

Have your passport at the ready!

"Always be ready to have the time of your life."
Tatum Thatcher

"Photographer Yousuf Karsh and his wife were having lunch with astronaut Neil Armstrong after a photo session. Armstrong politely questioned the couple about the many different countries they had visited. "But, Mr. Armstrong," protested Mrs. Karsh, "you've walked on the moon. We want to hear about your travels." "But that's the only place I've ever been," replied Armstrong apologetically."
'The Little Brown Book of Anecdotes'

"I'd rather have a passport full of stamps than a house full of stuff."
Anonymous

Know you can

We are "the little engine that could".

"Inside my empty bottle I was constructing a lighthouse while all the others were making ships."
Charles Simic

"My father used to say that it's never too late to do anything you wanted to do. And he said, 'You never know what you can accomplish until you try'."
Michael Jordan

Recognize your greatness

"Men are made stronger on realization
that the helping hand they need
is at the end of their own arm."
Sidney J. Phillips

"Opportunity is missed by most people
because it is dressed in overalls
and looks like work."
Thomas Edison

Affirm your worth

"Try to discover
The road to success
And you'll seek but never find,
But blaze your own path
And the road to success
Will trail right behind."
Robert Brault

"The same boiling water that softens
the potato hardens the egg.
It's about what you're made of,
not the circumstances."
Unknown

Expect the unexpected

"If you do not expect the unexpected
you will not find it,
for it is not to be reached by search or trail."
Heraclitus

"I like to photograph someone before they
know what their best angles are."
Ellen Von Unwerth

"An idea that is not dangerous is unworthy
of being called an idea at all."
Oscar Wilde

"It's what you learn
after you know it all that counts."
John Wooden

Take a vacation

"A vacation is having nothing to do
and all day to do it in."
Robert Orben

"Real events don't have endings,
only the stories about them do."
James Galvin

"If you don't live in another country
for a while, you have no perspective
on your life or your own country."
Mark Twain

Give yourself an "A"

"Become a beacon of light.
Every day expect to win something."
Andre Reed

"Sometimes, the most brilliant and intelligent
students do not shine in standardized tests
because they do not have standardized minds."
Diane Ravitch

Make humor part of each day

"I love people who make me laugh.
I honestly think it's the thing I like most,
to laugh. It cures a multitude of ills.
It's probably the most important thing
in a person."
Audrey Hepburn

"Laughter is timeless.
Imagination has no age.
And dreams are forever."
Walt Disney

"If you love the law and you love good sausage,
don't watch either of them being made."
Betty Talmadge

Be curious

"You can teach a student a lesson for a day;
but if you can teach him to learn
by creating curiosity, he will continue
the learning process as long as he lives."
Clay P. Bedford

"Get over the idea that only children
should spend their time in study.
Be a student so long as you still have something
to learn, and this will mean all your life."
Henry L. Doherty

Stop, look, listen

"When God sneezed,
I didn't know what to say."
Henny Youngman

"I question not if thrushes sing,
If roses load the air;
Beyond my heart I need not reach
When all is summer there."
John Vance Cheney

"In the name of God, stop a moment,
cease your work, look around you."
Leo Tolstoy

"The earth has music for those who listen."
George Santayana

Hop on a bike

"Happiness is a direction, not a place."
Sydney J. Harris

"Just as we teach our children how to
ride a bike, we need to teach them
how to navigate social media and
make the right moves that will help them.
The physical world is similar to the virtual
world in many cases. It's about being aware.
We can prevent many debacles
if we're educated."
Amy Jo Martin

Play the Money Game to win

"Money never remains just
coins and pieces of paper.
Money can be translated into
the beauty of living,
a support in education, or future security."
Sylvia Porter

"You are an irresistible magnet, with the power
to attract unto yourself everything that you
divinely desire, according to the thoughts,
feelings and mental pictures
you constantly entertain and radiate."
Catherine Ponder

Master snow angels

"Sunshine is delicious, rain is refreshing,
wind braces us up, snow is exhilarating."
John Lubbock, 'Recreation, The Use of Life', 1894

"Probably the happiest period in life
most frequently is in middle age,
when the eager passions of youth are cooled,
and the infirmities of age not yet begun;
as we see that the shadows,
which are at morning and evening so large,
almost entirely disappear at midday."
Eleanor Roosevelt

Play in the rain

"The best thing one can do when it's raining
is to let it rain."
Henry Wadsworth Longfellow

"Wherever you go,
no matter what the weather,
always bring your own sunshine."
Anthony J. D'Angelo, 'The College Blue Book'

"Letting go means to come to the realization
that some people are a part of your history,
but not a part of your destiny."
Steve Maraboli

Just say

"Everything you can imagine is real."
Pablo Picasso

"Attitudes are contagious.
Are yours worth catching?"
Dennis and Wendy Mannering

"If you don't think every day is a good day,
just try missing one."
Cavett Robert

As you watch the sunset
let the mind set too

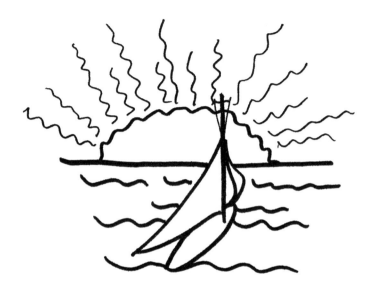

"Life is like sailing.
You can use any wind to go in any direction."
Robert Brault

"Twenty years from now
you will be more disappointed by the things
you didn't do than by the things you did.
So throw off the bow lines.
Sail away from the safe harbor.
Explore. Dream."
Mark Twain

Ponder
the expanding universe

"The goal of life is to make your heartbeat
match the beat of the universe,
to match your nature with Nature."
Joseph Campbell

"It's not that I'm so smart,
it's just that I stay with my problems longer."
Albert Einstein

"Change the way you look at things
and the things you look at change."
Wayne W. Dyer

Lick the beaters

"I'll try anything once, twice if I like it,
three times to make sure."
Mae West

"I hate television.
I hate it as much as peanuts.
But I can't stop eating peanuts."
Orson Welles

"Sometimes you need to talk to a
three year old just so you can
understand life again."
Unknown

Enjoy the many forms
of abundance

Abundance isn't just stuff
- it's beauty and joy and love

"The true definition of science is this:
the study of the beauty of the world."
Simone Weil

"Whatever we are waiting for
- peace of mind, contentment, grace,
the inner awareness of simple abundance
- it will surely come to us,
but only when we are ready to receive it
with an open and grateful heart."
Sarah Ban Breathnach

Give someone an amazing day
...be free with acknowledgements

"Appreciation is the highest form of prayer,
for it acknowledges the presence of good
wherever you shine the light
of your thankful thoughts."
Alan Cohen

"They say beauty comes from a spirit
that has weathered many hardships in life and
somehow, continues with resilience.
Grace can be found in a soul
who ages softly, even amid the tempest.
I think the loveliest by far is the one
whose gentle heart bears a hundred scars
from caring, yet still finds a way to
pick up the lamp, one more time,
to light the way for love."
Susan Frybort

Savor your
favorite chocolate

"Chocolate is happiness that you can eat."
Ursula Kohaupt

"I prefer to regard a dessert
as I would imagine the perfect woman:
subtle, a little bittersweet,
not blowsy and extrovert.
Delicately made up, not highly rouged.
Holding back, not exposing everything
and, of course, with a flavor that lasts."
Graham Kerr

"Chocolate is the answer.
Who cares what the question is."
Unknown

Be a contribution

"In about the same degree as you are helpful,
you will be happy."
Karl Reiland

"Be of service. Whether you make yourself
available to a friend or co-worker,
or you make time every month to do
volunteer work, there is nothing that harvests
more of a feeling of empowerment
than being of service to someone in need."
Gillian Anderson

"No act of kindness, no matter how small,
is ever wasted."
Aesop, 'The Lion and the Mouse'

Add value to your life

"All of us need to grow
continuously in our lives."
Les Brown

"Live your truth. Express your love.
Share your enthusiasm.
Take action towards your dreams.
Walk your talk.
Dance and sing to your music.
Embrace your blessings.
Make today worth remembering."
Steve Maraboli

Ask and be open to what comes

"Ask for what you want and be prepared to get it!"
Maya Angelou

"First, remember that you can think whatever you
please. Your thoughts are under your control.
No one else can think for you. Think creatively
so that you have more desirable experiences.
Even though you may not fully accept or understand
these statements yet, begin to put them into
actual application for yourself…start right now."
Betty Simmons, Coaching Magic

"Set a goal so big that you can't achieve it
until you grow into the person who can."
Unknown

When life deals you lemons...

"There comes a time in your life, when you walk away from all the drama and people who create it. You surround yourself with people who make you laugh. Forget the bad, and focus on the good. Love the people who treat you right, pray for the ones who don't. Life is too short to be anything but happy."

José N. Harris

"Sometimes walking away has nothing to do with weakness, and everything to do with strength. We walk away not because we want others to realize our worth and value, but because we finally realize our own."

Unknown

Unlock the mystery
...metamorphosize

"In the end, we won't remember
the most beautiful face and body,
we'll remember the most beautiful
heart and soul."
Anonymous

"Until one has loved an animal,
a part of one's soul remains unawakened."
Anatole France

"Spirituality does not come from religion.
It comes from our soul."
Anthony Douglas Williams

Live large

"Here's to the crazy ones.
The misfits, the rebels, the trouble makers, the round
heads in the square holes, the ones who see things
differently. They're not fond of rules and they have
no respect for the status quo. You can quote them,
disagree with them, glorify or vilify them.
The only thing you can't do is ignore them,
because they change things. They push the human
race forward and while some may see them
as the crazy ones, we see genius.
Because the people who are crazy enough
to think they can change the world
are the ones who do."
Jack Kerouac

Say 'thank you' for every day

"A birthday is just the first day of another
365-day journey around the sun.
Enjoy the trip."
Unknown

Be an inspiring example

"Be an opener of doors
for such as come after thee."
Ralph Waldo Emerson

"If you inherently long for something,
become it first.
If you want gardens, become the gardener.
If you want love, embody love.
If you want mental stimulation,
change the conversation.
If you want peace, exude calmness.
If you want to fill your world with artists,
begin to paint.
If you want to be valued, respect your own time.
If you want to live ecstatically,
find the ecstasy within yourself.
This is how to draw it in,
day by day, inch by inch."
Victoria Erickson

Splash in the pool

"Ships don't sink because of the
water around them.
Ships sink because of the
water that gets in them.
Don't let what's happening around you
get inside you and weigh you down.
Refuse to sink!"
Unknown

"Don't cry because it's over,
smile because it happened."
Dr. Seuss

Count the colors in a rainbow

"If you awake every morning with the thought
that something wonderful will happen in your life
today, and if you pay close attention,
you'll often find that you're right."
Unknown

"Every so often your loved ones will open the door
from Heaven, and visit you in a dream.
Just to say "Hello" and to remind you
they are still with you, just in a different way."
Matt Fraser

"The way I see it, if you want the rainbow,
you gotta put up with the rain."
Dolly Parton

"Take me, I am the drug;
take me, I am hallucinogenic."
Salvador Dali

Be authentic

"Before you can inspire with emotion,
you must be swamped with it yourself.
Before you can move their tears,
your own must flow.
To convince them, you must yourself,
believe."
Winston Churchill

"The privilege of a lifetime
is to become who you truly are."
C. G. Jung

"Only the truth of who you are,
if realized, will set you free."
Eckhart Tolle

Feel the wind in your hair

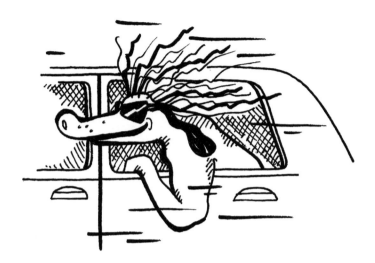

"And forget not that the earth
delights to feel your bare feet
and the winds long to play with your hair."
Khalil Gibran, 'The Prophet'

"Following all the rules
leaves a completed checklist.
Following your heart
achieves a completed you."
Ray Davis

Expand your mind

"You must constantly ask yourself these questions: Who am I around? What are they doing to me? What have they got me reading? What have they got me saying? Where do they have me going? What do they have me thinking? And most important, what do they have me becoming? Then ask yourself the big question: Is that okay? Your life does not get better by chance, it gets better by change."
Jim Rohn

"Shoot for the moon. Even if you miss, you'll land among the stars."
Norman Vincent Peale

Fun moments become memories

"You gotta have fun.
Regardless of how you look at it,
we're playing a game.
It's a business, it's our job,
but I don't think you can do well
unless you're having fun."
Derek Jeter

"I only drink champagne on two occasions:
when I'm in love and when I'm not."
Coco Chanel

Wear a wacky hat

Go bold
...make a style statement

"Creative minds always have been known
to survive any kind of bad training."
Anna Freud

"Why are you trying so hard to fit in,
when you're born to stand out?"
Oliver James

Fulfill your dreams

"You know you're in love when you
can't fall asleep because reality
is finally better than your dreams."
Dr. Seuss

"If you don't build your dream,
someone will hire you to build theirs."
Tony Gaskins

"All our dreams can come true -
if we have the courage to pursue them."
Walt Disney

"Reach high, for stars lie hidden in your soul.
Dream deep, for every dream
precedes the goal."
Ralph Vaull Starr

"A dream is your creative vision for your life
in the future. You must break out of your cur-
rent comfort zone and become comfortable
with the unfamiliar and the unknown."
Denis Waitley

"Miracles start to happen when you
give as much energy to your dreams
as you do to your fears."
Anonymous

"You may say I'm a dreamer,
but I'm not the only one.
I hope someday you'll join us.
And the world will live as one."
John Lennon

It's ok to be goofy

"Limitations live only in our minds.
But if we use our imaginations,
our possibilities become limitless."
Unknown

"Realistic people who pursue practical aims are
rarely as realistic or practical in the long run of
life as the dreamers who pursue their dreams."
Hans Selye

"Give a man health and a course to steer,
and he'll never stop to trouble about
whether he's happy or not."
George Bernard Shaw

An apple a day...

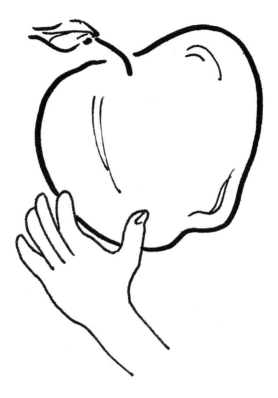

"Good apple pies are a considerable part
of our domestic happiness."
Jane Austen

"Anyone can count the seeds in an apple,
but only God can count the number
of apples in a seed."
Robert H. Schuller

"If you have an apple and I have an apple
and we exchange these apples, then you and I
still each have one apple.
But if you have an idea and I have an idea
and we exchange these ideas,
then each of us will have two ideas."
George Bernard Shaw

Singin' and dancin' in the rain

"Life isn't about
waiting for the storm to pass;
it's about learning
to dance in the rain."
Vivian Greene

"I only sing in the shower.
I would join a choir,
but I don't think my bathtub
can hold that many people."
Jarod Kintz

"When you truly sing, you sing yourself free.
When you truly dance, you dance yourself free.
When you walk in the mountains or swim in the sea,
again, you set yourself free."
Jay Woodman

"The moment in between what you once were,
and who you are now becoming,
is where the dance of life really takes place."
Barbara de Angelis

Give thanks

"For each new morning with its light,
For rest and shelter of the night,
For health and food, for love and friends,
For everything Thy goodness sends."
Ralph Waldo Emerson

"Not what we say about our blessings,
but how we use them,
is the true measure of our thanksgiving."
W. T. Purkiser

"How glorious a greeting
the sun gives the mountains!"
John Muir